T0158529

The Melting Pot

Maggie Ogunbanwo
Photography Huw Jones

For Jean Hefina,
for helping me see and love Wales.

GRAFFEG

Contents

Starters & Soups

Mains

Desserts & Drinks

Cover photo: Quick Chicken Jollof Rice
© Huw Jones, recipe page 96.

Foreword

It gives me great pleasure to write this foreword to a hugely important book in reflecting the diverse Wales in which we live.

As the Black Lives Matter campaign came to the forefront of everybody's minds, Maggie Ogunbanwo approached the Welsh Government's Food and Drink division with the idea of creating a practical resource developed by the BAME community and made available to all.

This is the result and it is a wonderful achievement. Collated and edited by Maggie, the recipes alone are worth the cover price but this is so much more than a cookbook. It is a showcase of contemporary Wales through the eyes of those within the BAME community who are making a valuable contribution to the Welsh food and drink industry.

Whether it be Wayne Booth's tantalising Caribbean Salt Fish Fritters, the Aberystwyth Syrian Dinner Project's delicious Fattoush salad or the mouth-watering Quick Chicken Jollof Rice created by Maggie herself, this book opens our eyes to the fantastic diversity of Wales and how these communities and businesses enrich our lives and support local suppliers.

Our culture in Wales is rich and varied and our nature is one of open arms and welcome – of providing a sense of belonging, of having pride in our 'cynefin'.

This book reinforces those views and I encourage you all to try the recipes, read the stories and appreciate our diverse country.

Lesley Griffiths, Minister for Environment, Energy and Rural Affairs, Welsh Government.

Introduction

Black and ethnic minority communities often settle in unfamiliar places but quickly begin to reach out in the way they know best, and that is often through the language of food.

So, we seek to tell you the stories of our minority communities all across Wales with this delightfully colourful and varied collection of recipes. We have recipes covering Africa, like our quick Nigerian-inspired jollof – jollof rice is made differently by everybody's grandmother and has been the cause of great debate: the Jollof Battles between Nigeria and Ghana. We have included a quick starter jollof recipe in this volume so you can begin to grasp what it is that causes so much debate in West Africa.

Moving to the Caribbean, we feature quintessential saltfish fritters, our Syrian community speak to us through three traditional courses and we include contributions from Bangladesh, Kenya, Zimbabwe, Bali, and more. A veritable melting pot!

I am particularly drawn to the Balinese turmeric cold brew coffee because of its colour and the health benefits derived from turmeric. I must confess I am not a fan of drinking turmeric in its raw form, so this is such a pleasant and novel way to get more turmeric into your diet.

I encountered falafels when I first came to live in the UK and realised that we had the equivalent in Nigeria in the form of akara, or blackeye bean fritters, but ours are beaten with a

little onion, chilli and salt to produce a light fluffy fritter covered in a brown crispier outer that is just divine.

As you try out these recipes, I hope you begin to understand a little bit more about the diverse flavours and all the variety that the BAME community brings to our communities all over Wales.

Maggie Ogunbanwo

Three-Bean
Bajan
Croquette

Earl is often hosting parties at home for friends with lots of dietary needs and is always asked to make his Barbados sauce. He usually serves this with fishcakes or chicken, but the bean croquette is a nice addition that incorporates the fruity, citrusy Bajan seasoning to give a spicy base to the croquette before adding the balancing coconut flavours of the sauce.

Three-Bean Bajan Croquette
by Charmaine and Earl Smikle

Makes 6 | Prep time 20 minutes | Cook time 30 minutes

Ingredients

1 medium onion, finely chopped

1 carrot, finely chopped

1 celery stick, finely chopped

30g Bajan seasoning

200g kidney beans (tinned)

200g black-eyed peas (tinned)

25g vegetable bouillon powder

200g gram flour

1 medium egg, beaten, or 50ml water for vegan version

Dried breadcumbs

200ml vegetable oil

200g butternut squash

200g sweet potato

200g swede, chopped

1 courgette, chopped

1 pepper, chopped

1 tablespoon Patak's curry paste

2 spring onions

Method

- Place the butternut squash and sweet potato in an oven at 180°C/160°C Fan/Gas Mark 4 and bake for 45 minutes until soft. Allow to cool, then peel off the skin and roughly chop.
- Peel and roughly chop the swede into even pieces. Add the chopped swede to a medium saucepan with the chopped courgettes and peppers and cover with cold water. Bring to the boil and simmer for 14-16 minutes, until cooked through. Drain and mash well – this may be easier in a food processor.
- Strain the beans and blend in a food processor to a rough paste.
- Heat a medium frying pan with a drizzle of oil, add the onions, celery and carrots and cook until softened.
- Add all the mashed vegetables (butternut squash, sweet potatoes, courgettes, peppers) to the onion, celery and carrot mix and stir in.

Three-Bean Bajan Croquette

- Add the Bajan seasoning, vegetable bouillon and 100g (half) of the gram flour and cook for 5 minutes whilst stirring.
- Add the curry paste and bean mixture to the pan and mix well.
- Remove the pan from the heat and leave to cool.
- When the mixture is cool, you can shape it into small balls or croquettes.
- Put the remaining gram flour, beaten egg or water and panko breadcrumbs in three separate bowls. Roll the croquettes in the gram flour, dip in the beaten egg, then roll in the panko breadcrumbs.
- Heat oil in a large, non-stick frying pan and shallow fry the croquettes on a low-medium heat for 4-5 minutes, turning frequently for an even, golden colour. Drain on kitchen paper and serve with Earl's Kitchen Vegan Barbados Sauce or Scotch Bonnet Chilli Chutney.

Vegan Ajiaco Soup

This is a traditional vegan winter soup in Colombia. I learned the recipe from my father-in-law, who is a retired chef and added his own touches, because it reminds me of home and the family gatherings there. Guascas, the Columbian herb, gives this soup its delicious flavour. It is more difficult to find in the UK but can be replaced with dill – all other ingredients are available in most markets.

Vegan Ajiaco Soup
Isabelle, Women Connect First

Serves 4 | Prep time 15 minutes | Cook time 45-55 minutes

Ingredients

2 tablespoons olive oil

1 onion

3-4 garlic cloves, crushed

2 large carrots, peeled and sliced

800g vegetable stock

2 bay leaves

3g dried guascas (quickweed), stems removed

2 medium baking potatoes

3 medium red potatoes, cut into small chunks

400g sweet potatoes or medium new potatoes, cut into small chunks

1 teaspoon sea salt

Ground pepper, to taste

2 ears fresh corn, cut into thirds or quarters

3 spring onions, sliced

2 tablespoons fresh chopped coriander

Fresh lime juice

Vegan sour cream

½ cup capers

2 avocados, peeled and sliced

Vegan Ajiaco Soup

Method

- In a large soup pot, heat the oil over medium heat and sprinkle with salt. Add diced onion and sauté for about 3-4 minutes.
- Add the crushed garlic and peeled and sliced carrots and sauté for 2-3 minutes.
- Raise the heat to high and add the vegetable stock, peeled and sliced red potatoes, baking potatoes, guascas, bay leaves, salt and pepper. Once the soup starts to boil, turn the heat to medium-low and allow to simmer with the pot covered. Cook for about 20-30 minutes, until the potatoes are starting to break down. Using a fork, mash some potato pieces against the side of the pot to thicken the soup.

- Now add the sweet or new potatoes, corn cobs (cut into 3-4 pieces), sliced spring onion and coriander. Simmer for 15-20 minutes, until the potatoes are tender and the corn is cooked. Mash a few more potatoes, if preferred. Check the seasoning and add more salt and pepper if needed. Remove the bay leaves.
- Remove from the heat and add the lemon juice. Serve hot with sour cream, capers and avocado slices.

Buy dried guascas online, it makes all the difference.

Stuffed Kibbeh

Everything we cook comes from traditional recipes with some modifications made by my mum. Kibbeh is considered the national dish of many Middle Eastern countries, including Syria, and uses bulghur wheat, finely chopped onions and red meat – this recipe uses beef – to create a delicious fried croquette.

Stuffed Kibbeh
by Latifa Al Najjar, Syrian Dinner Project
Serves 10 | Prep time 40 minutes | Cook time 20 minutes

Ingredients

Stuffed kibbeh:

1kg lean minced beef

1.5kg fine bulgur

1 large onion

2 tablespoons salt, or according to taste

1 teaspoon all spice berries

¼ teaspoon cumin

1 teaspoon black pepper

Oil, for deep frying

The filling:

1kg minced beef

2 large onions, finely chopped

2 tablespoons ghee/clarified butter

1 tablespoon salt

1 teaspoon spices and pepper

1 tablespoon molasses

¼ cup pine nuts

Method

- Wash the bulgur twice and set it aside in a colander for half an hour.
- Put the bulgur and the minced beef for the kibbeh with the rest of the ingredients into a food processor and process twice to a sausage-like consistency, adding a little iced water if necessary to encourage movement.
- Put the processed mix in a bowl, cover with clingfilm and put it in the fridge for an hour or more.

For the filling:

- Place the ghee in a saucepan and heat on high.
- Add the finely chopped onions with the minced beef, salt and pepper and the molasses, until softened.
- Mix in the pine nuts, then take off the heat and allow to cool completely.

Stuffed Kibbeh

- Take out a section of the dough and shape it into a hollow rugby ball shape with one end open.
- Fill with a little of the kibbeh and seal shut with a little water if needed.
- In a frying pan, heat enough oil to shallow fry the stuffed kibbeh a few at a time. Allow room to turn them.
- Serve hot or cold with a side salad with caraway dressing or as a snack.

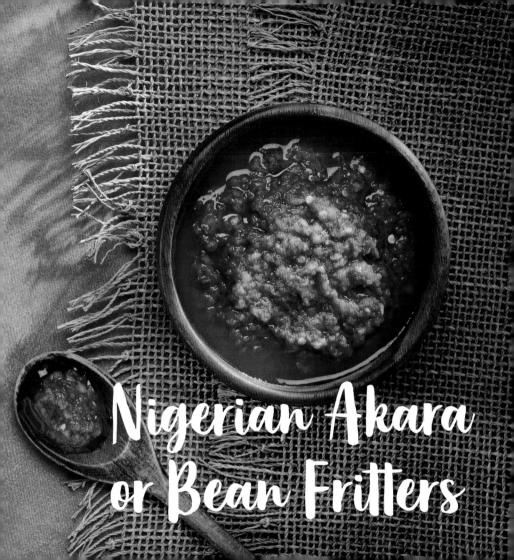
Nigerian Akara or Bean Fritters

Akara are bought on the roadside in the mornings as a snack, used as breakfasts during Ramadan and sold with dundun (fried yam slices) for lunch. My all-time favourite memories of akara are having them with ogi (a fermented white maize custard) for breakfast. The fluffiness of the inside of the akara with its burst of chilli is just so good. Oloyin or Nigerian brown beans are traditionally used and can be found in ethnic food stores. I most commonly use the white beans with black eyes that you can get in most supermarkets.

Nigerian Akara or Bean Fritters
by Maggie Ogunbanwo

Makes 6 | Prep time 25 minutes | Cook time 20 minutes

Ingredients

500g black-eye/brown beans

½ onion, very finely diced

3 small mixed sweet peppers (red, orange, yellow), very finely diced

500ml vegetable oil, for deep frying

1 teaspoon salt, or according to taste

Akara is a street food that is popular all over Nigeria. Everybody's mum and nain claims to have the best recipe and I have adapted this from what I saw being made as a young girl.

Nigerian Akara or Bean Fritters

Method

- Soak the beans in water overnight.
- The next day, drain the beans and rinse thoroughly.
- Blend the beans to a paste using as much water as is needed to achieve this.
- Put the blended paste through a fine mesh sieve and drain the water until a thick, dry paste is achieved. You may need to stir the paste to encourage this process.
- Add the drained paste together with the finely diced onions and peppers and the salt into a large bowl, mixing well until combined.
- Heat the oil in a wok or deep frying pan and gently drop one heaped tablespoon at a time into the oil. Do not overcrowd the pan.
- Fry for 3 minutes on one side and for 2 minutes on the other, until golden-brown.

- Remove with a slotted spoon and serve as a snack or a light lunch with a salad garnished with caraway dressing.

Tips
- In order to achieve a crispy outer shell with a fluffy interior, start with the oil on high heat then turn it to medium so the akara do not brown too quickly without getting cooked inside.
- To achieve a lighter, fluffier akara, whisk the mixture vigorously for a few minutes with a hand or electric whisk before frying.
- Try different beans for the same idea with interesting taste and texture variations.

Caraway
Dressing

Caraway Dressing
by Maggie Ogunbanwo

Makes 155g | Prep time 10 minutes

Ingredients

18g garlic

2g oregano

6g salt

50g olive oil

1 tablespoon caraway
seeds or ground
caraway

½ large lemon, juiced

3g black pepper

50g water

5ml Maggie's original
chilli sauce or any chilli
sauce

Method

- Place all the ingredients in a food processor and whizz on high until all mixed in.
- Refrigerate and pour over a mixed leaf salad as required.
- It will last for 3-5 days in a tightly covered jar in the fridge.
- This is such a divine tasting dressing and could work well as a fish seasoning.

A salad dressing inspired by the cooking of Tunisia.

While I am a very instinctive cook a lot of my recipes are influenced by my mother and grandmother, who were both excellent cooks and mixed their different cultural experiences into their cooking. My caraway dressing is especially influenced by my research and cooking for African pop-up restaurants in Penygroes, North Wales. Caraway is not a herb that you often see mentioned in recipes, but here adds such a distinctive flavour that leaves you wanting more and works well with any salad.

Sweet Potato and Coconut Soup

Traditionally, sweet potato is a staple in our Southern African diet. Sweet potatoes are boiled, roasted, mashed or made into a soup for a delightful lunch. The coconut milk is used to enhance the flavours and give a thick, rich texture, while the chilli sauce completes the soup for a spicy and satisfying meal. For our family, this makes a great starter during the festive season or a delightful, satisfying lunch dish on cold days. In the days before Christmas, in a house full of family visiting from Botswana and Australia, the soup is made in two large pots for mild and hot flavours.

Sweet Potato and Coconut Soup

by Valerie Creusailor

Serves 4 | Prep time 25 minutes | Cook time 50 minutes

Ingredients

4 tablespoons Naga chilli olive oil or olive oil

200g red onion, finely chopped

500g sweet potatoes, peeled and chopped

2 garlic cloves, crushed

7.5cm fresh root ginger, peeled and finely chopped

400ml coconut milk

2 teaspoons coconut flakes

600ml water

½ teaspoon chilli sauce or chilli flakes

½ teaspoon salt

½ teaspoon freshly ground black pepper

Once served, the silence as everyone devours it speaks volumes. It is always the nods and satisfying grunts that make this a favourite.

The key ingredients can be sourced from any supermarket or from fruit and vegetable shops. Goch Naga Chilli Sauce is available online (an unsweetened chilli sauce can be used as an alternative) and soy milk can be used to replace coconut milk if preferred.

Method

- On low heat, fry the onions for about 5 minutes. Add the sweet potatoes and fry for 5 minutes or until golden-brown.
- Add the garlic, ginger, chilli sauce or chilli flakes, water and coconut milk.
- Mix the coconut flakes, salt and pepper and add.
- Bring the mixture to a fast simmer, then reduce the heat. Cover the pan and simmer for 30-40 minutes.
- Cool for 5 minutes before blending the mixture in a food processor. Return the soup to the pan for another 5 minutes before serving.

Saltfish Fritters

Saltfish Fritters
by Wayne Booth

Serves 4-6 | Prep time 35 minutes | Cook time 30 minutes

Ingredients

125g salt cod or other saltfish, soaked in water overnight (water changed several times)

100g self-raising flour

250ml water (you only need enough for a thick paste)

¼ red pepper, diced

¼ green pepper, finely diced

¼ onion, finely diced

½ Scotch bonnet chilli, seeded and finely chopped (½ green chilli for a milder version)

Freshly ground black pepper

Vegetable oil, for shallow frying

Method

- Drain the soaked salt cod and cook in boiling water for 20-25 minutes or until the fish is flaky and tender. Drain the salt cod and flake the flesh, removing the skin and pin bones.
- Tip the flour into a bowl and stir in enough cold water to make a thick paste. Stir in the salt cod, red and green peppers, onion and Scotch bonnet chilli and season with freshly ground black pepper.

This is a traditional Jamaican recipe which I grew up with and have eaten all my life. A favourite memory of mine is making it for some friends and the look of delight on their faces when they first tasted them. The balance of flavours from the salty saltfish to the heat from the Scotch bonnet makes the fritters exceptional. Saltfish fritters are made for birthdays, weddings and any type of celebration – it's a dish that won't be around for long when people start eating at the Caribbean banquet. All of the ingredients can be sourced at your local supermarket or any Asian supermarket.

- Heat 2.5cm/1in of vegetable oil in a deep, heavy-based frying pan until a breadcrumb sizzles and turns brown when dropped into it. (CAUTION: hot oil can be dangerous. Do not leave unattended.)
- Carefully place spoonfuls of the batter into the hot oil and fry for 2-3 minutes or until the fritters are crisp and golden-brown (you may need to do this in batches). Remove from the pan with a slotted spoon and set aside to drain on kitchen paper to remove any excess oil.
- Serve with sweet chilli sauce or hot pepper sauce for an authentic Caribbean taste.

Welsh Callaloo with Fried Dumplings

This is a Welsh version of Jamaican callaloo, a style of dish that would be made for a cooked breakfast or brunch on a Saturday or Sunday or for special occasions. We replaced the callaloo with spinach, chard or kale, which are perfect local ingredients to give the dish the same wholesome flavours as the callaloo you would find in Jamaica. When my husband had a rather special birthday recently, I made this as one of the canapés and everyone was delighted with it. The dumplings, split in half with a little of the spinach mixture topped with a sliver of chilli, made a tasty bite to eat.

Welsh Callaloo with Fried Dumplings

by Yve and Lascelles Forrest

Makes 4 | Prep time 30 minutes | Cook time 45 minutes

Ingredients

3 medium organic onions

2 cloves organic garlic

½ organic red pepper

3 tomatoes, chopped into 8 pieces

3-4 sprigs fresh thyme

400g of organic spinach washed.

2 tablespoons coconut oil

225g organic self-raising flour

225g Y Felin 80% hand sieved wholemeal flour (or a self-raising wholemeal flour – if using this, please omit the baking powder)

4 teaspoons baking powder

10g sea salt

4 tablespoons coconut oil

We can't get fresh callaloo so this is the closest we have to it in Wales. You could use chard, beetroot leaves or kale or whatever is in season to achieve the same style dish.

Method

- Finely chop the onions, chop the pepper and crush and chop the garlic.
- Put the coconut oil in a skillet or saucepan and fry the onions on a medium heat for 3 minutes, then on a lower heat for a further 10-12 minutes until the onions are translucent. Add the thyme and the garlic and sauté for a further few minutes.
- Meanwhile, chop the tomatoes and add them to the skillet. Continue cooking the mixture down for a further 5 minutes.

To make the dumplings:
- Put all the flours, baking powder and salt into a mixer and mix gently to combine.
- Add just enough water to make a dough (this should not be too soft or too firm).

Welsh Callaloo with Fried Dumplings

- Kneed the mixture for 1-2 minutes, turn out onto a lightly floured surface, then kneed by hand for a further 1-2 minutes.
- Split the dough into 12 equal portions. Roll into a ball, then flatten and turn the edges into the middle whilst moving the dough around in a full circle. Finish by slightly depressing the mixture in the middle.
- Put the coconut oil, just 2 tablespoons to begin with (adding more when necessary), into a skillet/ frying pan on a medium to low heat.
- Fry the dumplings slowly for about 5 minutes until golden on one side, flip for a further 5 minutes or more to get the other side golden, then stand the dumpling on its side in the pan. Do this until all the dumplings are cooked on all sides, about 15-20 minutes in total.

- Delicious as a starter – just half one dumpling and top with the spinach mixture – or serve 2-3 dumplings at a time with the spinach.

This is a vegan dish. You can make it pescatarian by adding some saltfish or mackerel.

Jamaican Curry Goat

This recipe is influenced by traditional Caribbean cooking, modified by my addition of coconut cream, which gives a tantalising flavour along with the traditional spices. Curried goat is a must at weddings and funerals in Jamaica and is therefore associated with celebrating life and the life of a dearly beloved. Christmas time is my favourite time of year to prepare all of my Caribbean favourites – we have a bountiful buffet and cooking starts from Christmas Eve. I always cherish these memories, with the family sniffing around the kitchen as the curried goat simmers!

Jamaican Curry Goat
by Bernie Davies

Serves 6 | Prep time 20 minutes | Cook time 190 minutes

Ingredients

1.25kg goat, trimmed, cubed and goat bones.

1 teaspoon medium dried pimento berries (all spice)

100g Jamaican curry powder

4 sprigs thyme, to taste

3 cloves garlic, crushed

30g all-purpose seasoning, done to taste, based on salt tolerance

1 medium white onion, finely diced

1 medium red onion, finely diced

3 sprigs spring onion, finely chopped

½ sweet red pepper, chopped

½ sweet yellow pepper, chopped

½ sweet green pepper, chopped

1-2 Scotch bonnet (habanero) peppers, deseeded and chopped (to taste, based on spice tolerance – handle these with care, always wear gloves while handling Scotch bonnet peppers)

1 block coconut cream, diced

Method

- Wearing a pair of gloves, rub the curry powder, pimento, garlic, thyme and all-purpose seasoning into the goat meat, ensuring it's all evenly distributed, then leave to marinate overnight in the fridge.
- Remove the next day and allow to stand for about an hour.
- Place the meat mix into a large Jamaican Dutch pot on low heat to 'seal' the meat and cover with the lid. Check every 5 minutes, stirring the meat gently until all of the pieces have been sealed by the heat and no longer have the red colour of uncooked meat.
- Add hot water from the kettle by pouring around the inner circumference of the Dutch pot to prevent losing the spice on the meat. Never pour water on top of spiced meat at this stage.

Jamaican Curry Goat

The water level needs to be just above the level of the meat (an inch or so).

- Bring to a boil on high heat, then turn down the heat to medium to simmer. From time to time you may need to top it up with hot water until the meat is tender.
- My rule of thumb is that the meat is tender enough when you can cut into it with the side of a spoon.
- Keep the pan covered while cooking. Always check the water level does not go too low, thereby causing the meat to stick to the pan.
- When the meat is tender to taste, layer the top of the goat with the diced white and red onions, the chopped spring onions, the chopped mixed peppers and the chopped Scotch bonnet peppers – a bit like a carpet across it all. Cover and simmer, allowing the spices to seep downwards into the meat.

- Add the block of diced coconut cream so it melts quickly and simmer to the desired sauce level.
- Add extra all-purpose seasoning to taste if necessary.
- Serve with boiled rice or Jamaican rice and peas (kidney beans).

Chioma's Beef and Tomato Stew

This is my own creation based on a common stew eaten in every household across Nigeria and has a tantalising appearance when served. Usually a lunchtime delicacy, the nourishing aroma of garlic and ginger makes it unique. All ingredients are readily available.

Chioma's Beef and Tomato Stew
by Chioma Njoku

Serves 4-6 | Prep time 15 minutes | Cook time 1 hour

Ingredients

1kg beef, chopped

200g tomato purée

250g fresh tomatoes

50ml extra virgin oil

½ red onion, finely chopped

50g ginger

3 cloves garlic

20g Scotch bonnet chillies (use with caution, perhaps start with half)

100g red bell pepper

Salt, to taste

Seasonings:

½ teaspoon black pepper

2 bay leaves

1 tablespoon nutmeg powder

1 tablespoon curry powder

½ tablespoon dried thyme

2 beef stock cubes

Chioma's Beef and Tomato Stew

Method

- Season the chopped beef with the black pepper, bay leaves, nutmeg, curry powder, thyme and stock cubes.
- Add the seasoned chopped beef to a medium saucepan with enough water to cover and bring to the boil. Turn down the heat and simmer for 30 minutes, adding water if needed to prevent burning.
- Blend or process the tomatoes with the Scotch bonnets (if using), ginger, garlic and the non-chopped half of the onion.
- Place the blended mix above in a separate medium saucepan with the tomato purée and bring to the boil for 15 minutes, until the mix becomes dry without burning.

- Drain the beef into a bowl, saving any liquid, and put the empty saucepan back on the heat with the olive oil.
- When the oil is hot, add the drained beef and stir-fry with the other half of the chopped onion for 5 minutes.
- Now add the cooked tomato mix to the beef with some of the set aside beef stock, season to taste with salt and allow the stew to simmer for 10-15 minutes.
- The beef stew is ready to serve with white rice or boiled potatoes as a main meal.
- Beef can be substituted with chicken, fish or turkey, in which case cooking times will alter.
- You can make this dish vegan by using vegan stock cubes and any vegetables of your choice.

Efo Riro

This is a traditional dish common to the Yoruba people of south-west Nigeria, especially Lagosians, with some personal twists, especially the quantity of chilli used. I learned to make this dish from the age of ten and my favourite memory of preparing it was actually messing it up with some spices (thyme, curry, white pepper) not considered for use with soups like this in my culture. The whole family ate it while throwing jibes at me and that was a mistake I never made again! It is special to me due to its mixture of different seafoods and meats and can be eaten with anything from rice to starchy dough-like dishes like eba (particularly with Lagosians, as sometimes the water used to cook the crabs is used in making the eba to give the eba itself a flavour).

Efo Riro

by Derin Omole, Twale Cuisine

Serves 4-6 | Prep time 30 minutes | Cook time 1 hour

Ingredients

2 bunches (500g) fresh spinach (900g frozen spinach)

3 medium red bell peppers (tatashe)

2 Scotch bonnet chillies (rodo), or 1 or fewer for people with a mild tolerance

8-10 bite-sized pieces tripe (shaki), cow skin (pomo), cow leg, smoked turkey, beef, or assorted meats of your choice

225g king prawns (optional)

1½ onions

½ cup palm oil or preferred cooking oil (vegetable or sunflower oil are suitable substitutes)

300g fresh white fish or other seafood of choice, like crabs (optional)

100g smoked fish

1 tablespoon locust beans (iru) (optional)

1 tablespoon ground crayfish (or crayfish powder)

1 Maggi cube (or any stock cube of your choice)

Salt, to taste

Popular as 'soul food', efo riro can be consumed at home for lunch or dinner or served at events; it also makes a tasty vegetarian option without the meat/seafood.

Method

- First of all, if using any meat or chicken, season to taste and cook properly by boiling until tender. You can also use the grill to dry it a little (grilling is a healthier option to frying). Set aside.
- Wash your vegetables thoroughly with warm water and a bit of salt to get rid of any sand or dirt if using fresh vegetables. You can slice/chop them, but not too finely, or tear up the leaves with your fingers so as not to lose too much chlorophyll and retain the nutrients. If using frozen vegetables, defrost them as usual and ensure they are well drained to remove any excess fluid, as you don't want to end up with a watery efo riro.
- Blend the peppers and half the onion coarsely or finely (your choice) and set aside.

Efo Riro

- Chop the remaining onion and split into two portions. Pour the palm oil into a saucepan and heat for about 2-3 minutes until it lightens up (don't bleach palm oil), or use your cooking oil of choice until it is hot enough to fry (sauté) half of the chopped onions and the aroma of the onions is released. If using locust beans *(iru)*, pour in and fry these in the oil for about 1-2 minutes, until the aroma is released.
- Add in the blended pepper and seasoning cubes (Maggi cube), ground crayfish, the dried catfish (so it can soften while the pepper is drying out) and about half a teaspoon (2.5g) of salt and fry until thick and not too dry (just a little water content present).
- Add in all your cooked and grilled meat/chicken/ fish and allow to steam in the pepper sauce for 7-10 minutes, absorbing the pepper and any

The health benefits of efo riro can't be overemphasised, as green leafy vegetables are known to be a great source of vitamins and minerals and are rich in folic acid, calcium and iron. Palm oil and locust beans (iru) are rich in vitamin A and help to improve eye health. Any accompanying meat/fish or chicken is a great source of proteins too.

water content left in the pepper sauce. Taste the sauce and adjust the seasoning if need be.

- Add your washed and drained vegetables and the rest of the chopped onions and combine thoroughly by stirring the vegetables into the pepper sauce. Allow to simmer on low heat for about 5 minutes.
- Turn the heat off, but leave the lid on for the steam to cook it for another 5 minutes.
- Serve with your swallow of choice or any of the suggestions above.

Kousa Mahshi

Mahshi means stuffed, and we are very well known in the Middle East for different mahshi dishes. I have used the traditional recipe, but the topping is something I learnt from my mother while I was home for a visit a couple of years back. I love cooking this dish because it reminds me of all my family gathering for our dinners together. Of all the sorts of mahshi, my children prefer the courgettes, which I really find the easiest among them to prepare. I find the topping of fried garlic and mint really makes this dish outstanding.

Kousa Mahshi

Feryal A, Women Connect First

Serves 4 | Prep time 25 minutes | Cook time 1 hour

Ingredients

4 medium courgettes

200g long grain rice

100g minced beef

60g onion, finely chopped

1 teaspoon mixed spice

1 teaspoon turmeric

½ teaspoon salt and black pepper

500g tomato passatta

70g tomato purée

200-250ml water

1 tablespoon oil

3 cloves garlic, finely sliced

2g fresh mint sprigs, chopped

Method

- Wash the rice and soak it for 15 minutes. In the meantime, empty the insides of the courgettes. You can do this using an apple corer, but leave about ¼ in of flesh around the sides.
- Drain the rice and mix with the chopped onion, minced meat, salt, pepper, mixed spice and turmeric.
- Stuff the courgettes with the rice mixture.
- Mix the tomato passata with the tomato purée and add to a deep frying pan/skillet. Add the salt and pepper and bring to a boil.

This recipe could be made quicker using pre-cooked rice. You can make this a totally vegan recipe by omitting the minced beef.

- Once the sauce is boiling, turn down the heat and add the filled courgettes one by one into the pan. Bring back to the boil on high heat then turn down to medium and let the courgettes simmer for 40 minutes. Add water from time to time to prevent burning.
- Heat the oil in a frying pan and add the garlic, frying until golden, then add the chopped mint. Add this mixture to the courgettes.
- You can serve the courgettes with some yoghurt.

Green Beans in Tomato Sauce

Green Beans in Tomato Sauce
by Jenan Al-Shebibi, Women Connect First

Serves 4 | Prep time 15 minutes | Cook time 40 minutes

Ingredients

450g fresh green beans, rinsed and trimmed

1 tablespoon olive oil

1 large onion, peeled and minced

2 garlic cloves, peeled and diced

400g chopped tomatoes

1 teaspoon cumin

1 teaspoon paprika

½ teaspoon dried oregano

1 tablespoon sugar

Salt, to taste

Black pepper, to taste

1 tablespoon fresh parsley, chopped

½ teaspoon cayenne pepper

This is a very traditional salad used in Egypt as a side dish but can be served as a main during the Lent fasting.

It always brings back good memories of my mother when she was with us, especially during our holy month of Ramadan, and I have added a few ingredients that I learnt from her. The oregano and the sugar are extra ingredients which I feel give an enhanced taste to this dish.

Method

- In a saucepan, sauté the onion in olive oil over medium heat until tender, about 5 minutes.
- Add the minced garlic, stir and cook 30 seconds.
- Add the green beans, turn the heat to high and stir quickly for about 1 minute.
- Add the chopped tomatoes and enough water to almost cover the beans.
- Add the parsley, cumin, sugar, salt and pepper.
- Cover the pot and simmer on medium heat for about 25 minutes.
- If it seems too watery, cook uncovered for 10 minutes. There should be about a third to half the amount of liquid you started with.

Lamb Pilau Rice with Kachumbari Salad

Lamb Pilau Rice with Kachumbari Salad

by Justina John

Serves 4 | Prep time 40 minutes | Cook time 50 minutes

Ingredients

500g lamb fillet, cut into 5cm cubes

1 tablespoon salt

1 tablespoon ginger paste

1½ tablespoons garlic paste

1.2l water

2 tablespoons oil

1 tablespoon whole cumin seeds

1 tablespoon pilau masala, garam masala, or 1 cinnamon stick, 4 whole cloves,

5 cardamom pods, 6 whole black peppercorns

2 large onions, finely chopped

2 large potatoes, chopped into medium-sized pieces

1 large tomato, grated (optional)

400g basmati or long grain rice, soaked for 30 minutes and drained

¼ teaspoon ground coriander

¼ teaspoon ground cumin

1 handful fresh coriander, chopped (optional)

Kachumbari salad:

1 red or white onion, diced

1 large tomato, diced

1 tablespoon lemon or lime juice

Pinch red chilli powder or any fresh chilli (optional)

Salt, to taste

Most elements of this recipe are traditional. The style of cooking is influenced by my late mother, but I also like to add my own twist to every dish I cook. Pilau rice is associated with celebrations, happiness and family back home in Tanzania and it is usually enjoyed during festivities and on Sundays after church, Christmas, Eid, and other celebrations, including my own Holy Communion. I remember the whole preparation as my aunties and sisters were sitting outside the house peeling onions, garlic and potatoes. The aroma was always very strong, as the spices were freshly prepared, and the garlic and spices are key to the dish. For a vegetarian alternative, the meat can be replaced with vegetables that can be cooked with rice.

Lamb Pilau Rice with Kachumbari Salad

Method

- Place the lamb in a saucepan and rub with 1.4g of salt and 1 teaspoon each of ginger and garlic paste. Leave to marinate for a minimum of 15-20 minutes.
- Add the water to the marinated lamb and boil over medium to high heat for 20 minutes or until the lamb is cooked through. Strain the lamb, saving the stock.
- Heat the oil in a large saucepan over medium heat and add the cumin seeds and pilau masala or the cinnamon, cloves, cardamom and black peppercorns. Allow the spices to crackle for approximately 1 minute.
- Add the onion to the spices and sauté until brownish and translucent.

Tip: Start by soaking the rice and marinating the lamb. While that is going on in the background, continue with the other preparation.

- Add the potatoes and stir until they turn a brownish colour.
- Add the tomato, the remaining ginger and garlic pastes and stir well. Leave to cook on high for approximately 2 minutes.
- Lower the heat and add the cooked lamb. Stir well.
- Add the drained rice to the saucepan along with all the reserved lamb stock, the remaining salt, the ground coriander, cumin and the fresh chopped coriander. Cover the saucepan with the lid and cook over medium heat for 15-20 minutes or until the rice is cooked and all the stock has been absorbed.
- **Kachumbari salad preparation:** Mix all the ingredients in a bowl and serve as an accompaniment to the pilau rice.

Fattoush Salad

Fattoush Salad

by Latifa Al Najjar, Syrian Dinner Project

Serves 4 | Prep time 20 minutes

Ingredients

1 romaine lettuce

2 cucumbers

2 tomatoes

1 red pepper

1 green pepper

4 radishes

1 bunch scallions or 1 yellow onion

5 tablespoons olive oil

1 tablespoon salt

2 tablespoons sumac

2 tablespoons dried mint

1 slice toasted pita bread

1 sprig fresh mint, to taste

Method

- Roughly chop all the ingredients (apart from the bread) and mix together with the olive oil, salt, sumac and dried mint.
- Garnish with shredded pitta slices and fresh mint.

I remember coming home from school to the amazing smell of my mum's cooking and our gatherings around the table during the month of Ramadan, where the fatoush salad was the centrepiece of the table.

Spicy Beans
(Ewa)

This brings back fond memories of growing up in Nigeria and of ewa day, where you either smothered the spicy beans in gari, a powdery flour common across Nigeria, or made a drinking porridge of the gari with water, loads of sugar and ice-cold water. This was our favourite as kids and we savoured the hot and cold contrast with the beans.

Spicy Beans (Ewa)
by Maggie Ogunbanwo

Serves 4 | Prep time 10 minutes | Cook time 3 hours

Ingredients

225g blackeye beans

2 medium fresh tomatoes

1 medium red onion

½ red bell pepper

2 tablespoons tomato purée

1 teaspoon Naija This & That seasoning (or all-purpose seasoning)

1 teaspoon olive oil (palm oil traditionally used)

2 teaspoons dried ground crayfish (fish sauce can be used)

1 stock seasoning cube

1 teaspoon salt

1 teaspoon Maggie's chilli sauce or any chilli pepper, to taste

1 tablespoon sugar (optional)

Method

- Soak the blackeye beans overnight in water or according to the instructions on the packet.
- Drain and discard the water and rinse the beans thoroughly.
- Place the beans in a slow cooker with twice the amount of water, cover and leave to cook on high for 2½ hours. This can be done overnight.

If cooked on the cooker, hob times will vary and the amount of water needed will vary also.

- Meanwhile, process together the tomatoes, red onion, red bell pepper and dried crayfish (if using) in a blender or food processor to a fine paste. You may need to use a little liquid from the cooked beans to move the process along.
- Drain the cooked beans, saving the drained liquid. Place the cooked beans into a medium saucepan with the blended paste, vegetable stock cube and tomato purée and stir well.
- Bring to the boil on high heat, then turn the heat down to a simmer.
- Add the Naija This & That seasoning, the olive oil and 175g of the liquid set aside from cooking the beans, stir well and crush some of the beans against the side of the pan with the back of the ladle to make a thicker sauce. You can also take

Spicy Beans (Ewa)

out a bit of the bean mix, blend and add it back into the pan to obtain similar results.

- Add salt and hot chilli pepper according to taste and leave the lid off for a bit to reduce the sauce and thicken it further to a thick curry.
- Serve hot with roti/flatbread or fried plantains/dodo.

Tips:

- Any other type of bean can be used but taste and cooking times will vary according to the bean.
- You could try making this using tinned beans, but you may need to cook them until they are a little softer. This will cut out the 2½ hours cooking time in the slow cooker.
- Red onions give this dish a characteristic sweet taste, but if unavailable then white onions can be used and 5ml sugar added.
- Palm oil is traditionally used instead of olive oil.

Roti

Roti (Unleavened Bread)
by Maggie Ogunbanwo

Makes 12 | Prep time 10 minutes | Cook time 20 minutes

Ingredients

500g plain flour

250g hot water

1 teaspoon salt

1 tablespoon vegetable oil

Method

- Place the flour, salt and oil into a large bowl. Add the hot water and mix until a smooth, soft, but not sticky dough is achieved.
- Form the dough into 12 golf-sized balls and set aside on a floured surface.
- With floured hands, flatten a ball and roll out using a floured rolling pin on a floured surface to make a 22cm circle.
- Place a flat or griddle pan on high heat and brush the surface with oil using a pastry brush. When steaming hot, place a rolled-out roti onto the hot griddle pan, cooking until bubbles start to appear on the surface. Using a pair of tongs, turn the roti over and cook on the other side until dry and bubbles appear. Each side should have lightly browned spots.
- Remove and place on a clean tea cloth and wrap to keep warm. Repeat until all the rotis are cooked and serve with spicy beans/ewa or a curry.

Quick Chicken Jollof Rice

Jollof rice is a West African institution and probably Nigeria's national dish. No West African celebration is complete without some version of jollof, in fact, to jollof is a trending word amongst Africans, meaning 'to enjoy'. Any jollof memory comes back to the uniting of Nigeria and Ghana (who always have wars over who makes the best jollof rice) against Jamie Oliver's rendition of this legendary African food. It created a social media storm and a brief friendship between the two countries. Jollof rice can be made without chicken for a vegan version – just add the vegetables of your choice.

Quick Chicken Jollof Rice
by Maggie Ogunbanwo

Makes 4-6 | Prep time 10 minutes | Cook time 50 minutes

Ingredients

450g long grain rice

4-8 chicken pieces

2 teaspoons Maggie's
Spice Up Chicken (or any
chicken spice)

225g whole tomatoes

50g tomato purée

110g medium onion

650–850ml chicken
stock

1 red bell pepper

1 teaspoon Maggie's
Roasted Chilli Sauce
with Balsamic

2 teaspoons salt, or to
taste

2 teaspoons Maggie's
Naija This & That mix
(or curry powder)

1 teaspoon black pepper

1 tablespoon ground
crayfish or fish sauce

2 tablespoons vegetable
oil

Quick Chicken Jollof Rice

Method

- Blend the onion, tomatoes and red pepper in a blender or food processor with a little of the stock to help the process and set aside.
- In a bowl, add the chicken pieces plus the Maggie's Spice Up Chicken and mix in well.
- Add the vegetable oil to a large saucepan and heat on high for 2-3 minutes. Now add the chicken pieces without overlapping and brown on each side in the hot oil, about 2-3 minutes on each side.
- Add the blended ingredients, tomato purée and enough stock to cover the chicken and ingredients to the pan, stir well and bring to the boil (10 minutes).
- Wash the rice in several changes of water or according to the manufacturer's instructions and drain in a colander.
- Add the drained rice and Maggie's Naija This & That Spice Mix or curry powder to the pan, stir and bring to the boil. Turn the heat to low, cover the pan firmly and leave to simmer.

Tip: You could use an 8oz can of chopped tomatoes instead of fresh tomatoes. Brown rice may be used but cooking times and the amount of water will vary. The crayfish is optional but is a traditionally used ingredient.

- Cook for a further 40 minutes until the rice is soft, stirring occasionally and adding more stock as required. To finish, add the crayfish or fish sauce and salt to taste and mix in well.
- The rice dish should be dry and the rice soft and plump, with the characteristic orange jollof colour.
- Leave to simmer for 2 minutes, then remove from the heat and serve hot with friend plantains and steamed mixed vegetables.

Groundnut Stew

Groundnut soup is influenced by a tradition that has been passed from generation to generation and which my mother passed on to me. After being taught the method, I was asked to prepare it on my own without any help, and, trust me, the look from my parents when it was ready said it all! I was so proud of myself. Peanuts, or groundnuts as they are called in my village, are the main ingredient and the traditional spice iru (ori), fermented locust beans, gives it a flavour no one can resist. It can be eaten anytime and is very cheap to make while not being time consuming. If needed, groundnuts can be substituted for peanut butter and the traditional spice (ori) can be replaced with a crayfish, chicken or beef seasoning cube or stock.

Groundnut Stew

by Omo Idegun, Wrexham Africa Society

Serves 4-6 | Prep time 10 minutes | Cook time 30 minutes

Ingredients

250g roast peanuts, puréed/peanut butter

120g onion, minced

30ml tomato purée

1 (400g) tin chopped tomatoes

½ teaspoon chilli pepper

1 vegetable stock cube

Salt, to taste

1kg cooked meat (beef, lamb, chicken or pork), cut into small cubes

Method

- Place the processed onion into a saucepan with the peanuts or peanut butter and stir-fry for 2-3 minutes.
- Add the tomato purée, chopped tomatoes, stock cube and chilli pepper and bring to the boil, stirring from time to time.
- Turn down the heat and simmer for 15 minutes.
- Add the cooked meat or vegetables and cook for a further 10 minutes until everything is hot. If the mixture gets too thick, add a bit of water to prevent it sticking to the pan.
- Serve hot with boiled basmati rice, pounded yam (*fufu*) or boiled yam.

This is a part of a main dish served in many parts of Africa under different names, including maffay.

Vegetable chunks, such as carrots, turnips, swede or potatoes, can replace meat in this recipe.

Vegan Spinach Lasagne

Vegan Spinach Lasagne
by Peter Merezana

Serves 4 | Prep time 30 minutes | Cook time 40 minutes

Ingredients

500g tofu

Black pepper, to taste

Salt, to taste

½ teaspoon dried mustard

½ teaspoon ground nutmeg

2 lemons

5 garlic cloves, peeled and diced

2 tablespoons olive oil

500g frozen spinach

250g lasagne sheets

50g plain flour

700ml unsweetened coconut milk

2 teaspoons dried oregano

50g margarine

200ml garlic and herb passata

This recipe makes use of vegan ingredients, but any of those could be switched for non-plant-based cheeses or meats. My recommendation would be Parmigiano-Reggiano.

Method

- Defrost the frozen spinach overnight in a bowl.
- **To make your vegan ricotta filling:** Add the garlic cloves, olive oil, half a teaspoon of salt, a generous pinch of nutmeg, a generous pinch of black pepper and the dried mustard into a blender.
- Cut the lemons in half and squeeze the juice into the blender. Blend until you have a smooth, creamy sauce.
- Add broken chunks of tofu and blend them until you have a well-combined and thick filling.
- **To make the creamy sauce:** Melt the margarine in a small saucepan, then add the flour and mix until you have a thick paste.
- Keep whisking as you add the unsweetened coconut milk until the sauce has thickened.
- **To make the tomato sauce:** Pour the garlic and herb passata into a mixing bowl. Add a generous

Vegan Spinach Lasagne

pinch of salt, a generous pinch of black pepper
and the dried oregano.

- In an ovenproof dish, assemble your lasagne.
Starting with a layer of lasagne sheets, then
spinach and tomato sauce, layer like this until
all the sheets, spinach and tomato sauce are
used up.
- Finish the lasagne with the creamy sauce, making
sure the pasta sheets are fully covered.
- Place into a preheated oven at 180°C/160°C Fan/
Gas Mark 4 for 30-40 minutes.
- Carefully remove from the oven once cooked and
cut into squares to serve.

Vegan Tuscan-Style Jamboree

These recipes, along with most of my cooking, were inspired by my childhood. Like most Londoners, my mother would work really long hours and left me in the hands of an Italian childminder, my aunty Ana, who was fond of food and would walk me through everything. I loved the hands-on aspect of putting together dishes and the pride of watching the family sat around a table enjoying our efforts. The most touching response was watching a toddler try to identify the many colours in the Tuscan-style jamboree, such as the black quinoa and avocado – two of my favourite, nutrient-rich ingredients in one dish. Her grandfather suggested that the dish be added to the school's curriculum as mandatory learning!

Vegan Tuscan-Style Jamboree
by Peter Merezana

Serves 4 | Prep time 5 minutes | Cook time 45 minutes

Ingredients

115g black quinoa

250g red kidney beans

200g sweetcorn

1 cucumber

1 large tomato

2 avocados

2 limes, quartered

handful of fresh coriander

1 handful of basil leaves

Black pepper, to taste

Method

- Rinse the black quinoa in a colander using cold water.
- Add the quinoa to a pan with 410ml of cold water. Leave uncovered and bring to a boil.
- Turn the heat down, cover with a lid and leave to simmer for about 20 minutes.
- Give the red kidney beans a rinse in a colander and pour into a different pot once drained.
- Drain the sweetcorn and add to the second pot. Bring to the boil, then turn off the heat and cover.
- Slice the cucumber into long, fine pieces.
- Find a large bowl and add the black quinoa, kidney beans, sweetcorn and sliced cucumber.
- Top with finely diced tomato. Season with salt and black pepper.

Born out of necessity, the phrase 'cucina povera' (the kitchen of the poor) is used often when discussing Tuscan food. Based on peasant traditions, the dishes tend to not be overly pedantic about aesthetic arrangement and waste no time in getting you to the taste. Colourful and inviting, the jamboree would be perfect for a summer party.

- Finely chop the avocados and add to the bowl.
- Garnish with lime quarters, coriander and basil leaves.

Vegan Un-beet-able Salad

Vegan Un-beet-able Salad
by Peter Merezana

Serves 4 | Prep time 5 minutes | Cook time 45 minutes

Ingredients

2 beets, cooked, peeled and diced

2 tablespoons olive oil

1 teaspoon salt

1 tablespoon sesame seeds

1 tablespoon pumpkin seeds

2 mint leaves

1½ packets vegan feta cheese

1 handful coriander

Method

- Slice the cooked and peeled beets into diced chunks and place into a bowl.
- Finely chop the mint leaves and add them to the bowl.
- Drizzle with oil and give them a good shuffle.
- Top with vegan feta cheese.
- *Voila* – ready to serve as desired for four diners.

I have used vegan feta for this example, but you can use another plant-based cheese of your choice.

Macher Jhol

Bangladesh is very rich in fish and they are used in many dishes because they are fresh and affordable. I learned this recipe from my mother before I got married and moved to the UK and cooking it reminds of home, the seashores and the fishmongers where we used to buy fish.

Macher Jhol

by Rehana N, Women Connect First

Serves 4-6 | Prep time 10 minutes | Cook time 40 minutes

Ingredients

5-6 pieces rohu fish (cod or halibut will also work)

1 large onion (half chopped and half in paste)

1 teaspoon ginger paste

1 teaspoon garlic paste

½ teaspoon turmeric powder

½ teaspoon chilli powder

½ teaspoon cumin powder

½ teaspoon coriander powder

½ medium cauliflower, cut into florets

1 medium tomato, cut into cubes

100g fresh runner or green beans (you can also use frozen)

Salt, to taste

60ml oil

Coriander, chopped

4-5 green chillies, whole (or milder if preferred)

Macher Jhol

Method

- Wash the fresh fish very well if this is needed.
- Rub the fish with half the turmeric and chilli powder and 1 teaspoon of salt.
- Put the oil in a deep saucepan on high heat and fry the fish for 2 minutes on each side. Remove from the pan and set aside.
- In the same oil, fry the chopped onions for a few minutes until they change colour.
- Add the ginger and garlic pastes, turmeric, chilli and coriander powders, cumin, salt, a little water and the onion paste to the onions.
- Cook the spices very well, adding water little by little. Add the cauliflower and beans and cook for a while. Add enough water to cover them, on medium heat. When the water has reduced a bit, add the fish pieces.

Coriander is added at the end to really bring out the flavours of the dish and the freshness of the fish. Potatoes and peas can be substituted for cauliflower and beans, but my family love the cauliflower.

- When the gravy is reduced, add the tomatoes and all the green chillies. Cook for another 5 minutes on a medium-low heat.
- Turn off the heat and add the chopped coriander.
- Cover with a lid and keep it on the stove for a while to rest and allow the flavours to mix in. The stove must be turned off.
- Serve hot with rotis, rice or potatoes.

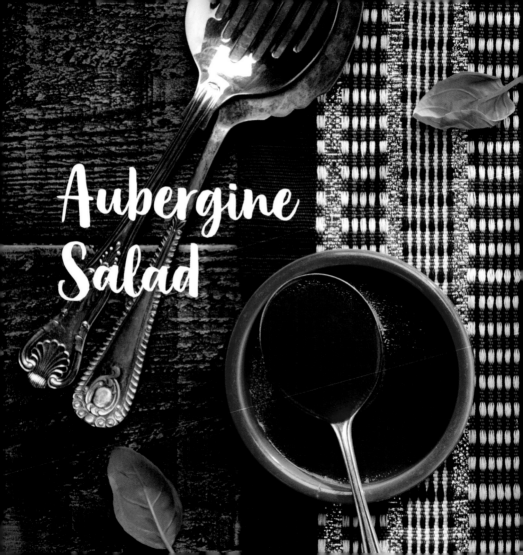

Aubergine Salad

This is a traditional salad you will find on most Iraqi menus with a few added ingredients that I have substituted to suit the taste of my family. It reminds me of all the good family gatherings around the dinner table, as this dish has been always been requested. The pomegranate sauce gives this dish a special flavour and can be found at most Asian supermarkets.

Aubergine Salad
by Women Connect First

Serves 4 | Prep time 60 minutes | Cook time 25 minutes

Ingredients

300g aubergine

1 large onion

1 large tomato

3 coloured peppers (only ½ of each is needed)

Cucumber, to garnish (optional)

5ml crushed garlic

Salt, to taste

Pinch ground cumin

15ml lemon juice

1 sprig mint leaves

1 sprig parsley

1 bunch basil

1 tablespoon pomegranate sauce

2 tablespoons olive oil

2 tablespoons tomato ketchup

2 tablespoons brown sauce

200g cherry tomatoes or radish

Aubergine Salad

Method

- Cut the aubergine into fingers, about the size of thick-cut chips.
- Place the aubergine fingers/slices into a bowl, mix with 1½ teaspoons of salt and set aside for an hour, covered.
- Uncover and rinse the aubergine fingers in tap water to remove the excess salt. Drain using a colander.
- Deep-fry the aubergine fingers for approximately 4 minutes (or more for a crispier version), remove from the oil and drain on a piece of kitchen cloth.
- Cut the onion, tomato, and 3 coloured pepper halves into similar size pieces or fingers.
- Stir-fry the onion, peppers and tomato slices with a little garlic to soften them.

- Mix all the vegetables with the aubergine, season with a little salt and ground cumin and set aside.
- In a separate bowl, mix the ketchup and the brown sauce with the olive oil, lemon juice and pomegranate sauce.
- Next, pour this mixture over the vegetables and mix in gently.
- Serve garnished with basil, parsley, cucumber and radish or plum tomato.
- Maple syrup can be used as a substitute for pomegranate sauce, but pomegranate syrup is readily available at Asian grocery stores.

Turnip and Lamb Stew

Turnip and Lamb Stew
by Women Connect First

Serves 4 | Prep time 20 minutes | Cook time 40-55 minutes

Ingredients

400g turnips, peeled and cut into cubes

500g lamb with bones, cut into chunks

4 tablespoons ground ginger

1 tablespoon ground garlic

2 medium onions, puréed

1 teaspoon ground red chilli

½ teaspoon ground coriander

½ teaspoon ground cumin

½ teaspoon garam masala

3 bay leaves

1 cinnamon stick

3 cloves

2 tablespoons vegetable oil

2 green chillies

1 teaspoon tomato purée

1 (400g) tin chopped tomatoes or 150g whole tomatoes

Method

- In a heavy-based pan, add the lamb chunks/pieces, ginger, garlic, puréed onions, tomatoes, chillies and all the spices with 200g of water.
- Let it cook on medium heat for 30-45 minutes, until the meat is cooked and the water is nearly dried.
- Next, add the oil and cook for a few minutes, stirring constantly.

This is a winter dish that is very popular with my family members back in Pakistan, where we used to gather around the table in the very cold evenings and enjoy the company and the food. Warming and filling, this is a very traditional way of cooking – simple and easy – with the chilli and cilantro adding to the taste.

- Add the turnips with 100g of water and cook until they are tender, mashing some of them to thicken the sauce. Serve hot.
- This is a thick, dryish curry, so if you want it thicker you could cook the turnips in a separate pan, mash a few and add them to the lamb mix when you add the oil.

Plantain
Cheesecake

My father, Earl, and I were looking to develop a plantain-based recipe because we'd managed to get lots from the local greengrocer. We had a bit of a challenge trying to do something different and delicious but opted for a cheesecake with a sweet and sticky glaze. I'd recommend visiting local greengrocers and ethnic food stores for their wide variety of products and the best of what's in season. If you're struggling to find plantain, banana could make for a good substitution.

Plantain Cheesecake
by Charmaine and Earl Smikle

Serves 8 | Prep time 1h 30 minutes | Cook time 60 minutes
Glaze Prep time 35 minutes | 30 minutes to cool

Ingredients

For the filling:

450g cream cheese (room temperature)

2 large ripe plantain (very important: make sure you use very ripe plantains, not green plantains)

4 medium eggs

250g honey

1 teaspoon vanilla

For the base:

200g digestive biscuits

50g unsalted butter, melted (plus extra to grease the tin)

Glaze:

120ml water

200g caster/granulated sugar

180-220g half-ripe plantains, puréed until smooth

60ml double cream (room temperature)

½ teaspoon vanilla extract

Method

- **To make the base:** Butter and line a 23cm loose-bottomed tin with baking parchment.
- Put the digestive biscuits into a plastic food bag and crush to crumbs using a rolling pin.
- Transfer the crumbs to a bowl, then pour over the melted butter.
- Mix thoroughly, until the crumbs are completely coated with butter. Tip them into the prepared tin and press firmly down into the base to create an even layer.
- Chill in the fridge for 1 hour to set firmly.
- **To make the filling:** If the plantain is not soft enough to purée then microwave it for 2-5 minutes or until soft and allow to cool.
- Position an oven shelf in the middle of the oven and preheat to 180°C/160°C Fan/Gas Mark 4.

Plantain Cheesecake

- Mix the room-temperature cream cheese with the puréed/mashed plantain, eggs, honey and vanilla until thoroughly combined (you can use a cake mixer or hand mixer), about 2 minutes.
- Pour the mix into the biscuit-lined tin.
- Place into the oven for 1 hour, depending on your oven, until firm.
- Remove from the oven and allow to cool before placing in the fridge for a minimum of 3-4 hours, but preferably overnight.
- Once completely set, you can remove it from the tin.
- **For the glaze:** In a large saucepan over medium-high heat, add the water and sugar. Bring to the boil, stirring constantly to dissolve the sugar.
- Turn the heat down to medium and allow the mixture to come to a light amber colour without stirring. Instead, swirl the pan

around occasionally to make sure the mixture caramelises evenly. (This can take a while, around 25 minutes. Be patient!)

- Remove the pan from the heat and add the puréed plantain. Stir until combined and the bubbling has stopped – it should be a deep, rich, amber colour. If too light, put it back on the heat and stir for a few minutes. Be careful, the caramel will bubble vigorously whilst adding the plantain.
- Remove from the heat and gradually pour in the double cream, stirring until combined.

The cheesecake needs to cool before placing it in the fridge for a minimum of 3-4 hours, but preferably overnight.

Balinese
Turmeric Coffee

My grandmother in Bali makes a 'health shot' every day using turmeric. My husband and I wanted to create a coffee using our favourite cold brew method with a Balinese influence, so we combined them and created our turmeric cold brew coffee. I love this recipe because it combines a traditional Balinese ingredient and processing method with my love for good coffee, as well as the yellow tinge of the drink. The earthy, nutty flavour of fresh turmeric really shines through and blends with the smooth, bold flavour of cold brew coffee.

Balinese Turmeric Coffee

by Intan Permata

Serves 4 | Prep time 15-18 hours | Cook time 25 minutes

Ingredients

50g high-quality arabica coffee, medium roast, coarsely ground (the same as for a French press or cafetière)

40g fresh raw turmeric

250ml whole milk

50g demerara sugar (or to taste)

Method

Prepare the cold brew concentrate:

- Put the coffee into a French press jug and add 400ml of cold water. Gently stir with a clean spoon. Leave to bloom for 30 minutes, then gently stir again. Ensure all the grounds are saturated.
- Cover the jug with cling film and leave at room temperature for 15-18 hours, depending on your preference and schedule.
- Strain the coffee. You can either gently push down the plunger from your French press or (if you want a cleaner coffee) you can pour it through a paper coffee filter. Do not squeeze the grounds too much to extract every drop of water – this will extract bitterness from the coffee. You will lose around 20% of the water you added as it is absorbed by the coffee.

Balinese Turmeric Coffee

For the best fresh turmeric, a market is usually your surest bet. If you don't drink dairy, oat milk works well (use a bit more than if it was normal milk).

- Discard the grounds and add 350ml of cold water to your cold brew concentrate. Now you have your cold brew coffee base!

Prepare the blend:

- Scrub the turmeric clean in cold water and roughly chop it. Be careful – it stains everything very easily! Either blend it with 40ml of cold water in a small food processor and then strain the pulp through a fine cotton cloth, using all your strength to squeeze out the juice, or, if you have a juicer, juice the turmeric and then add 40ml of cold water. I still recommend straining it through cloth after juicing, as it will still have a lot of pulp.

- Mix the turmeric juice, cold brew coffee base, milk and sugar in a jug. Stir until all the sugar is dissolved.
- Chill until ice cold. When ready, pour into a glass and sip on your delicious turmeric cold brew!
- Experiment with different coffee and different quantities of turmeric, milk and sugar. You can also drink the cold brew on its own, or with oat milk, ginger etc.

You can make more of the concentrate and turmeric juice by multiplying the amounts. They will keep in the fridge for up to 7 days, just make sure you stir the turmeric juice well before you use it.

Kanafeh

Kanafeh is a traditional dessert from the Middle East – this recipe is made using shredded filo dough, grated mozerella and a sweet syrup. It has special significance for me as the dessert served at family meals during the month of Ramadan.

Kanafeh

by Latifa Al Najjar, Syrian Dinner Project

Serves 8 | Prep time 25 minutes | Cook time 30 minutes

Ingredients

450g shredded filo dough (kanafeh/kataifi), chopped into small pieces

450g grated mozzarella cheese

200g room-temperature butter

Syrup ingredients:

2 cups sugar

1 cup water

½ teaspoon lemon juice

1 tablespoon rose water

1 tablespoon blossom water (mazaher)

Crushed raw pistachios, for garnish

You can find any unusual ingredients online or at Turkish or Asian grocers.

Method

- Preheat oven to 180°C/160°C Fan/Gas Mark 4.
- Mix the butter and kanafeh and rub it in well.
- Put a layer of the kanafeh mixture in a greased and lined oven dish, then put a layer of mozzarella cheese then another thin layer of kanafeh mixture. Continue layering, finishing with a layer of kanafeh.
- Place the dish in the bottom of the preheated oven.
- Cook for 20 minutes and finish off under the grill for 10 minutes; be careful not to let it burn.
- Meanwhile, make the syrup. Place the sugar and water in a small saucepan over medium heat and stir until the sugar dissolves and starts to thicken.
- Remove from the heat and allow to cool slightly before adding the rose and blossom waters. Stir in and set aside.
- Take the kanafeh out from under the grill and pour the syrup over it. Sprinkle with crushed pistachios to garnish.
- Cut into portions and serve.

Lemon Sunshine Cookies

Lemon Sunshine Cookies
by Maggie Ogunbanwo

Makes 22 | Prep time 15 minutes | Cook time 15 minutes

Ingredients

300g plain flour

10ml baking powder

½ teaspoon grated lemon rind

207ml condensed milk

Pinch salt

200g unsalted butter

½ teaspoon lemon juice

100g caster sugar

Icing sugar, for dusting

Method

- Sift the plain flour, baking powder and salt into a bowl.
- Place the butter and sugar into the bowl of a cake mixer and cream thoroughly, about 3-4 minutes.
- Add the condensed milk to the butter and sugar mix and beat until combined.
- Add the sifted flour mix to the butter, sugar and condensed milk mix with the lemon juice and rind and beat until mixed through.
- Line a large baking tray with greaseproof paper.
- Roll teaspoonfuls of the mix into 1-inch balls and place on a baking tray, widely spaced apart.
- Flatten the cookie dough with a fork to about ¼ in thick.
- Bake at 170°C/160°C Fan/Gas Mark 3 for 12-15 minutes.

I prepared these lemon sunshine cookies with and for the students at Ysgol Pendalar in Y Ffor and the memory of the way in which the students took on the tasks and viewed their end products always delights me. The fresh, zesty taste of warm lemons makes these a great snack with a paned (hot drink) or tipple!

- Remove from the oven and cool on a tray. Sprinkle lightly with icing sugar, *et voila*!

Banana and Walnut Breakfast Smoothie

Banana and Walnut Breakfast Smoothie

by Valerie Creusailor

Makes 2 | Prep time 10 minutes

Ingredients

150g orange segments

90g banana, peeled

150ml soya or skimmed milk

25g walnut pieces (or oats, raisins, pumpkin seeds or sunflower seeds)

1 teaspoon chilli jam or clear honey

150g natural yogurt

Method

- Place all the ingredients into a blender or food processor and blend until smooth and frothy.
- Pour into glasses and serve.

Oats, raisins, pumpkin seeds and sunflower seeds can be used as alternatives to walnuts.

This recipe was influenced by a busy home/work life and 'birthed' in our kitchen to ensure a healthy start to the day. It's quick and easy and our bananas never go to waste. The walnuts and chilli jam give great texture and delicious fruity aromas. Ideal for breakfast, it's especially lovely on hot summer days with a handful of crushed ice, and for summer barbeques or other festivities it can be served with fresh mint leaves and/or a dash of a good liqueur for an exotic touch. Goats' milk and/or skimmed milk can be used as an alternative. Goch chilli jams are available online or low-sugar chilli jams and honey are available in most supermarkets or local honey suppliers.

Maggie Ogunbanwo

Maggie Ogunbanwo's Maggie's: An African Twist to Your Everyday Dish operates from The Red Lion in the village of Penygroes in North Wales, surrounded by the beautiful Snowdonia countryside. Its roots, however, are deep in African soil, passed down through generations of instinctive but highly gifted culinary masters.

Maggie's influences flow from her *mam* and *nain* (mum and grandmother in Welsh) and are extended through contact with and work in environments with West Indian, Caribbean, Indian, Italian, Mediterranean and Latino foods. They continue to grow and meld, with an additional Welsh touch added to the mix, widening Maggie's international scope to tantalise a range of taste buds. As well as her passion for food and cooking, Maggie is committed to the quality and support of local providers.

Huw Jones

Huw Jones is a food photography specialist based in Newport, South Wales. His specifically designed studio is amongst the best equipped in the UK, with all dishes prepared and photographed on site using the highest-standard industry equipment.

Huw's stunning images showcase Gilli Davies's recipes in the Graffeg's Flavours of Wales and Flavours of England series, as well as the range of seasonal cookbooks from Angela Gray's Cookery School.

André Moore

Head Chef André Moore was born in Cardiff to a multi-cultural family and brought up in a melting pot of different cultures, foods and flavours. Both his father and stepfather Mike (a keen cook) come from Merchant Navy backgrounds and are responsible for introducing him to a host of new and exciting world ingredients from an early age. Taking this as his inspiration, he extensively travels, picking up new ideas and flavour combinations on the way.

Now with more than 25 years' experience of professional cooking, André splits his time between cooking for the Wales rugby team and working with Huw Jones producing perfectly presented food photography for a list of global clients.

Metric and imperial equivalents

Weights	Solid		Volume	Liquid
15g	½oz		15ml	½ floz
25g	1oz		30ml	1 floz
40g	1½oz		50ml	2 floz
50g	1¾oz		100ml	3½ floz
75g	2¾oz		125ml	4 floz
100g	3½oz		150ml	5 floz (¼ pint)
125g	4½oz		200ml	7 floz
150g	5½oz		250ml	9 floz
175g	6oz		300ml	10 floz (½ pint)
200g	7oz		400ml	14 floz
250g	9oz		450ml	16 floz
300g	10½oz		500ml	18 floz
400g	14oz		600ml	1 pint (20 floz)
500g	1lb 2oz		1 litre	1¾ pints
1kg	2lb 4oz		1.2 litre	2 pints
1.5kg	3lb 5oz		1.5 litre	2¾ pints
2kg	4lb 8oz		2 litres	3½ pints
3kg	6lb 8oz		3 litres	5¼ pints

Thanks

Well done to all the contributors for responding to my requests for information and near perfection.

Thanks to Caroline Hannah for spurring me on and pointing me in the direction of the fab Graffeg publishing team, Peter Gill, designer Joana Rodrigues, editor Daniel Williams and to Huw Jones photographer and André Moore chef and stylist. Also to Andrew Martin and Elaine Luke for encouraging comments at all stages.

To my family, for their honest feedback when they had to be taste testers. And thanks to Karen of Lavender and Lovage and Ileri Ogunbanwo for personally testing out several of the recipes in the book.

The Melting Pot – World Recipes from Wales. Published in Great Britain in 2021 by Graffeg Limited.

Edited by Maggie Ogunbanwo copyright © 2021. Food photography by Huw Jones copyright © 2021. Food styling by André Moore. Prop styling and post-production by Matt Braham. Designed and produced by Graffeg Limited copyright © 2021.

Graffeg Limited, 24 Stradey Park Business Centre, Mwrwg Road, Llangennech, Llanelli, Carmarthenshire, SA14 8YP, Wales, UK. Tel: 01554 824000. www.graffeg.com.

Maggie Ogunbanwo is hereby identified as the author of this work in accordance with section 77 of the Copyrights, Designs and Patents Act 1988.

A CIP Catalogue record for this book is available from the British Library.

The publisher gratefully acknowledges the financial support of this book by the Welsh Government.

ISBN 9781914079092

1 2 3 4 5 6 7 8 9